My Collie Girls & Me

*The True Story of Four Collie Girls
and the Blessings of God
Upon the Lady Who Loved Them*

MARILYN MARINELLI

My Collie Girls and Me
Copyright 2021 Marilyn Marinelli
Ocala, Florida
All rights reserved
First Edition 2022

Print ISBN 978-1-0878-7810-2
eBook ISBN 978-1-0878-5391-8

Cover & Formatting: Streetlight Graphics

This book is protected under US copyright laws. Any reproduction or other use is prohibited without the written permission of the author.

No part of this book may be reproduced, scanned, or distributed in any printed or electronic form without permission.

More books and Christian Ministry at
www.marinellichristianbooks.com

Introduction

I BELIEVE THAT MY STORY WILL be a blessing to you as you read about my collie girls and how God blessed me through their lives.

It is a story that shows you that no matter how hard things can get, with a trust and belief in God, all things are possible…That there are ways where there seems to be no ways and paths where there seems to be no paths.

Provisions are made if you believe and have faith that God cares. My collie girls are an example of this type of faith.

My hope is that you will come away from reading my book with a story to share with others. It's a story about love, faith, tears and great joy. It's all about the love of God given to me through Candy, Maggie and Ruby along with Buddy, Kody, Snowball, Crystal, Sammy and my newest "Collie Girl", Nellie.

I pray that when you see or have a special needs dog that you won't give up because there is hope. If you seek, you will find. Trust God to lead you.

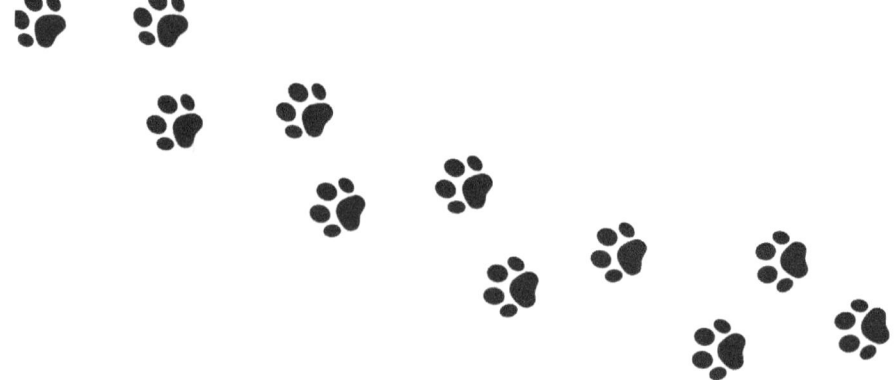

Table of Contents

Introduction ... iii
Chapter One ... 1
Chapter Two ... 23
Chapter 3 ... 38
Chapter Four ... 51
Conclusion ... 59
About the Author ... 61
Selected Poetry By Marilyn Marinelli ... 63

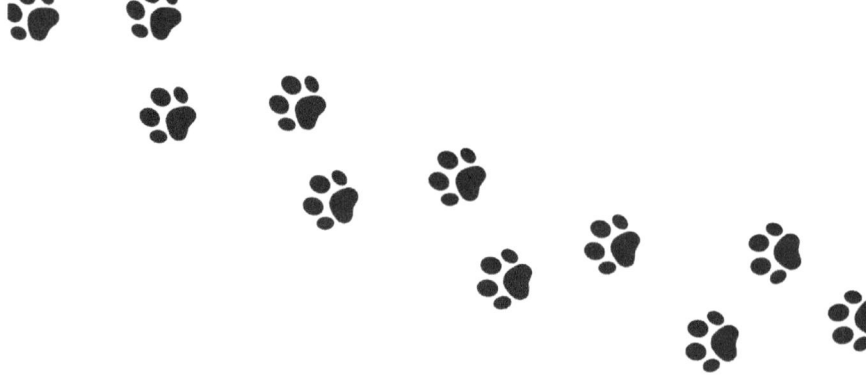

Chapter One

My Christmas Gift Of Love

Candy, My First Collie Girl

No, it is not Christmas yet, but I have a story to tell you about my first collie girl, so sit back and relax and know that all things are possible if you believe.

It was a trying time in my life. I experienced a burn out. I felt exhausted but finally started gaining strength. I needed something special to happen in my life. Little did I know that God had a plan. You see I was standing in my living room and all of a sudden God showed me something.

I saw a collie puppy with a red bow around its neck sitting at my front door, only the puppy wasn't really there. Yet, it seemed so real that when my husband came home from work, I told him what I saw and said, "If one day, when you come home from work and see a collie puppy sitting at our front door with a red bow around its neck, just take it inside." Well, of course he laughed. Days went by and no puppy sitting at my front door with a red bow around its neck.

Laugh if you will. But things started to happen. My husband and I went to a business fair where there were many tables set up with people selling things. One table we stopped by there were men selling puppies. The thing is, he didn't have any with him. He said, "tell me what kind of puppy you would like and I can get one for you. It will cost you $100 down and $300 more when you get the puppy." Well, I looked at my husband and said, "What do you think?" He was in agreement with me so I told the man I wanted a female collie puppy sable with some black around her neck. We gave him the deposit and went our way.

Another factor that was involved in our decision was the landlord. We were renting a wonderful home with a fenced backyard and three fruit trees… So, the next hurdle was to ask the landlord if he would be against us having a dog. Right away he said that it would be all right with him. Wow! What a relief.

I was working at the time so it wasn't going to be a big deal coming up with the $300 to pay for the puppy. We had already put $100 down. But a month or so passed and I left my job. I just couldn't keep up with the pace of going to work and running a family. There went the $300 we needed for the puppy.

As days passed, I was speaking with my dad on the phone and never mentioned the puppy or that I needed any money to purchase it. My dad, who never ever gave us any money, said to me that he wanted to give us a check to help us out financially. I told him no that we were all right and that he didn't have to give us any money. We went back and forth for a while and he said all right he wouldn't send any money our way.

A few days passed and I went to get the mail. There was an envelope and in it was a check for $300 dollars. Like I said, I never told my dad about the puppy. He would never have given me money to get a dog and I never mentioned $300. But there it was, a check for $300 in my hand written to me from my dad. When my husband came home that night. I told him what had happened and asked him if maybe we should keep the money to help us get along or spend it on the puppy. He said, "let's get the puppy."

Like I mentioned previously, I had gone through a burn out and was very tired but slowly getting better. I worked some; I exercised and I started to gain strength.

But God knew my heart and I really needed a special friend. Christmas was almost here.

It was time to get the puppy. We had to meet the man that was selling puppies in the back of a storefront. We walked in the back door and it was fixed up as if you were outside. He said to me, "sit down I will be right back with your puppy." I sat down and he comes out with this pretty collie puppy and placed it in my lap. Yes, she had a red bow around her neck. Remember that I told you I saw a collie puppy with a red bow around its neck sitting at my front door? God showed me that she was at the door of my life, not of my house.

Well, we took her home a few weeks before Christmas,1987. The next day we all, as a family, tried to come up with a name. It was unanimous. Her name would be Candy.

Candy was my **"Christmas Gift of Love"** sent from God Above directly to me.

Candy, John And Me

This story doesn't end here. Candy and I had a wonderful life together. She was my best friend.

Life's Experiences

We moved Candy into our bedroom to sleep with us at night. During the day she would run like wild fire around the backyard. The days past and it was time for training. We spent a number of weeks going to training class. Every day Candy and I would go for walks. We would practice sit, stay, come, heal and other commands.

Candy had a very special friend. Her friend was Snowball, our special kitty cat. She was deaf but that didn't stop her and Candy from being friends.

Snowball

Snowball passed away after a while. She was special. She was a beautiful white Turkish Angora cat that a friend of mine found for me from his mailman.

Another cat friend entered our life after Snowball passed. We named her Crystal. She was a shorthaired white cat. Candy now had another friend.

Crystal Kitty

Candy now was about a year old and my husband and I decided to move from Fort Lauderdale, Florida to Wisconsin for his job. So come on Candy and Crystal, let's get in the station wagon and ride up to Wisconsin.

Bad Advice

My vet, at the time, told me to give them both a tranquilizer. That was really bad advice.

Crystal became very hostile and vicious. We couldn't get near her. Candy became very lethargic. This happened to both of them on just one pill for one day. That was it, no more pills for them. The rest of the days we had to travel were a blessing to them both. They traveled well and we were all happy.

We all settled in our new home in Oak Creek, Wisconsin. That's just outside of Milwaukee. There was a big yard with lots of trees. The street we lived on was a dead end with only 4 homes on it and a big field at the end of the street. There was one farmhouse up the road and one farmhouse behind us.

Not only did Candy have Crystal as a friend inside the house, but Candy had a puppy dog friend from across the street that would come by and visit. You see, my new friend Karen had 5 kids, a cat and a newly acquired puppy dog. She would let her dog out and tell it to go to the neighbor's yard and do its business. At least that is what she would say and we all would get a laugh because really it never happened. Her little sweet dog just came to visit from time to time.

John and Candy

Daniel and Candy

Me and Candy

Candy and the neighbors dog

Candy would love to play. She would catch a ball and just have fun with us. I would take her out for walks and rides in the car.

Singing With Candy

I wasn't working anymore and didn't know what to do. My husband suggested that I start to sing some praise and worship songs like they do in church. He hooked up a microphone and speakers in our house. I started to buy cassette tapes and play them and learn some songs to sing.

Candy would be there in the living room with me. I bought a lot of songs and added more each week or so until I would sing for an hour every morning before making lunch to share with my husband. We met for lunch every day.

Candy loved this hour of singing with me. She and I would play together while I sang fast songs. I would sing and throw the ball and she would catch it. What fun we had together. Then I would sing some slower songs and she would rest by me as I sang. She became what I called, "My Praise And Worship Dog." This time together helped me to practice singing.

They started a group at church to help teach people how to sing specials in their Sunday morning service. When I shared a song or two one evening, one of the ladies leading this group said, "How do you do this?" She was referring to how I sang and delivered the songs. Right away she asked if I would sing a song as a soloist in the church the following weekend. After that I sang at other churches and even lead the music in our own church that my husband and I started years later.

Once I made friends with a lady that lived across the street, she told me that she could hear me singing. I never realized that the P/A System would carry the music and me singing from my home out to others that lived nearby.

Candy, Little Kids And The Mail

One day I decided I would take Candy out to get the mail. It wasn't a long walk, just to the end of the driveway. I would tell her to take a piece of the mail and she would carry it all the way back to the house, about 60 feet. We did this everyday and she felt important.

Then one day we went to get the mail, little Katie from across the street would come running out to see Candy and pet her. Everyday, Candy and I would get the mail and Katie would come out to pet her. But then it got to be another friend of Katie's that would come and join us and pet Candy. Then another kid, and another and then another showed up. After awhile I had about 9 or 10 kids coming to greet and pet Candy. Everyday as the kids went their way, Candy would carry a piece of mail back to the house. Yes, we lived on a dead-end street but the families there had a lot of children.

The seasons seemed to change fast in Wisconsin. Summer was a short but enjoyable time. Fall was a time where the trees were changing and it was glorious. Winter filled up with a lot of snow where Candy would come outside with my husband and I. We had so much fun playing in the snow. I even built a small snow lady. Here is a picture of me Candy and the snow lady.

Me, Candy And The Snow Lady

Of course, then spring came. It also was another beautiful time of the year.

Years passed and we move out of the house we were renting because the owner needed it back. We moved to an apartment across town but things didn't stop there for Candy.

Candy & Our Church

We started a non-denominational church in a little town called South Milwaukee. It was a storefront located between two bars. This is where I led worship and my husband preached. We were Co-Pastors. After church, we would take Candy to a local park and she would walk with us.

We also sponsored a church picnic when we lived in the rental home. It was for all of our church family. Candy had a lot of fun greeting and playing with all the children. Everybody loved Candy. That was before we moved to a near-by apartment.

I groomed Candy all the time. Here is a picture of how much hair I took off her to keep her looking good.

Me And Candy And Her Hair lol

Living in the apartment was short lived. My husband came home one day to say he was leaving his job and that he was offered a job in Florida.

Florida Here We Come

Leaving Wisconsin wasn't so bad. We were ready to leave the snow and the cold weather behind. We were glad to move where the weather was warmer. So come on Candy and Crystal kitty, we are going where the weather is warm.

The movers came and we were on our way to a new place called Ponte Vedra, Florida. Our new apartment was really very nice. There was a stream in the back and everything was nicely landscaped. We had two porches, one off the living room which was big and the other was smaller and off our dining area. We all settled in quite nicely and were ready for our new adventure.

Tough Times Ahead

Well, things didn't turn out as I had planned. I went to a chiropractor and was injured very badly. It took me 7 months to recover.

Candy and I hung out together everyday. I couldn't move my left arm very well at all. But, one day Candy brought me her fluffy football and wanted to play. I said, "Oh Candy I don't think I can play with you, but I will try and throw the football down the hallway".

We played like this everyday after that. It was a time of therapy for me to move my arm and Candy and I had so much fun.

I guess she became my therapy dog. One afternoon, I was getting a massage and was asked how I felt. I told the lady I felt faint, well she got me off the table and said, "we were going for a walk around the complex." She didn't even ask if she could take Candy. She just told me to get her leash; we were all going for a walk.

That became one of my first walks with Candy. Everyday, Candy and I walked the complex. We saw the ducks in a small lake and got the mail. She would carry one piece of mail in her mouth all the way back to our apartment. Remember she used to carry a piece of mail to our home in Wisconsin. We had many fun times together walking the complex, just

Candy and me. The therapy I needed at home was playing with Candy and throwing the fluffy football everyday and walking with her.

Candy At The Beach

Time went on and I became stronger and was healing. I met a friend and she wanted to go to the beach and I told her I would like to take Candy if that was all right. She said that they allowed dogs on the beach. So, Candy had her first experience going to the beach.

After that my husband, Candy and I would go to the beach. Candy and I would walk the shoreline and have a great time together. We would even walk when it was cold outside. Candy liked to chase the suds that rolled off the ocean and chase the birds. She was such a special friend.

Time passed and my husband decided that he needed to change jobs once again and we were going to move. I really didn't want to but we needed the money. So, we moved way up north to Minnesota.

A Loss But Also A Special Friend

We settled into a townhouse. All was o.k. except our cat, Crystal. She was not doing well. She had been diagnosed with diabetes when we lived in Florida. Time would pass and Crystal passed away in a veterinary clinic. John and I were with her and when she left this world, she put her paw out to me as if to say goodbye. Needless to say, it was a very sad time. I don't know how Candy felt about it but I am sure she must have wondered where Crystal was.

Sammy Joins The Family

I prayed to God that he would provide another white cat; one that looked more like Snowball, my Turkish Angora. Turkish Angora cats were expensive but God makes ways where there are no ways. He told me to wait. He said that when the cat is ready, he would let me know.

I know this is a story about Candy but God provides for his animals, as well. Only he would know what my Candy really was feeling and could provide for her as well as me in the loss of Crystal.

When You Least Expect It

Time passed and I decided to go shopping. You know… a lady thing. Never go to just one store; just kind of going on a hunt for clothes lol. It was close to my birthday so why not treat myself?

I got in the car and went into one store and then another and another. Each time I came out from a store it was if God was speaking to me to go to the humane society. I was like no way. I am shopping for clothes. Then I got into my car again and I was tremendously impressed of God to go to the humane society. It was like he spoke to me in a very soft voice. "I told you I would tell you when the cat for you was ready." I said to God, "Is that you? O.k. I will go to the humane society." It wasn't close to where I was shopping but I thought, "why not do what God was encouraging me to do?"

I arrived at the humane society. I had never been there before to really look around but I knew where it was located. I walked in and saw a round area with a bunch of kittens placed in it. There were also cats along the side of the wall that were in separate cages. Then there were also about 4 rooms with cats in them. I guess they were the cats that got along with each other. I stopped and looked at the kittens. Oh look, I thought, a pretty very small baby white kitten. This must be the one. One of the volunteers came over and asked if she could help me. I told her I wanted to see this little white kitty. She picked it up and we went into a little enclosed sitting area. She handed me the kitty and it screamed and screamed and screamed. I thought, "oh no! This couldn't be the one."

I thought, "Well this is a dead end." So, I figured, while I was there, I would go back and look at the dogs and puppies. After that I decided to go back to look at the cats again. Only this time I decided to just go into one of the rooms, look around and then leave.

But God had other plans. I stepped into the room with all these cats and one from across the room came strolling right up to me. It was a white Turkish Angora cat. Just at the time this cat reached me, a lady volunteer must have come in the room. She said to me, "Would you like to see this cat?" My first thought was, "No it was probably too old."

But then I changed my mind and told the volunteer, "Yes all right." She picked up the cat and took us both to an enclosed room. No sooner did I sit on the ledge that this little white fluffy cat jumped up on the ledge with me, then on my lap, then rolled over and purred. How could I miss God's provision and birthday present? This happened just around my birthday.

The lady volunteer told me this cat had been abandoned by the owner that it wasn't even a year old. She said that the neighbor found it all alone and brought it into the shelter. I was also told that the cat was already fixed. The adoption cost was $65. I told her I would take him.

I called my husband; told him I found this cat at the shelter and he said we would talk about it when he got home from work. "Oh, No Way", I said. "I will be bringing the cat home…No discussion about it."

You may be wondering why I am taking all this time to tell you about this special blessing for my birthday? Just keep reading and you will learn more about how this cat played a wonderful roll in Candy's life.

My New Furry Friend And Me

So off we went, my new furry friend and me. I was told I had to take it to the vet and I did before I got home. The vet told me that the cat wasn't fixed but had a receded testicle. All right, I thought. "I could help him with that." I left the vets office, me and my newfound friend and blessing from God.

When I got home, I placed the cat in the cat box on the table. I said, "O.k. God, if this is truly from you, let this cat get along with Candy." I let the cat out of the box and low and behold no problem with either one of them. They were friends from the start.

A Name Is A Name Is A Name

What to name this new addition to our family? God showed me a name in the Bible. It was Samuel. The name meant joy "Heard By God." I decided to name him Sammy. Yep, that would be his name. My husband had to get into the act and said that we ought to have an official name for the cat. He said that, "Sammy" was great but was just a short cut for a full name… so he proceeded to expand Sammy's name. Officially, the cat was crowned, Samuel Fuddlebee. He was Mr. Fuddlebee.

Candy had a new friend and Sammy had a new family. They loved hanging out together.

Candy and Sammy

The Next Move

I really wasn't happy in Minnesota. So, John, my husband and I decided to move back to Florida. He had to change his way in which he would work. But it would be a better place for us to live. He gave up his Sales Manager position and took a sales Rep position working for the same company. This time he would work from our Florida home.

So, there we were on the road once again heading for the same apartment complex we left a year ago in Ponte Vedra, Florida where we had lived previously before moving to Minnesota.

Candy and Sammy settled in once again and seemed to like it there. I was happy and Candy and I started to take our nice leisurely walks once again and checking on the ducks as we went over the little bridge to get the mail.

Sammy found some nice spots to hang out and we found a nice life together.

John and I would take Candy down to the beach for walks again which I think she really enjoyed. She would stop every time she saw someone walking with a small child and wait to say hello and get petted. Life was good.

I loved being back where the sun was shining. It was so much better than Minnesota where it was always cold, dingy, and a lot of snow. Yes, give me the sunshine and the beach and my husband and my doggy and kitty. I was a happy camper.

My husband and I would go fishing off the beach or on the pier and we would take long walks on the beach picking up seashells along the way. Candy was a beautiful collie with eyes that I called angel's eyes. Life was good.

Our First Home

We were going to move to a new home. It was built just for us. There was a beautiful lake in the back. We were finally homeowners. But Candy had a problem at a place we left her at when we went on vacation for only 4 days. When we picked her up, she had a fever of 104 and was not doing good. We took her to the vet and the fever left. But she had a terrible time walking.

We moved into our new home, but Candy still wasn't well. We helped her to walk and she just wasn't getting any better.

The Stray

There was a place in the back of our house that was lacking grass. It was right outside our bedroom window. What was this, I thought? I saw a dog leaving the back of our home and realized that this dog was sleeping outside our bedroom window. We finally were able to get the dog to come to us and we fed it and gave it shelter. It was a black short hair medium size dog.

I thought, "Where did it come from?" Then I remembered about a little over a year ago I saw a black momma dog and her black baby dog running along the lake in the back of our house. The momma dog was walking with the baby at one point and her puppy would run away from her and play in the water. Oh, she was so patient with her little one. She would wait and the puppy would come back to her and do it again and again. I found it so precious to watch. This dog by our bedroom window was the puppy that had grown up. What happened to the mother, I don't know but it became our responsibility to watch over this little one.

Eventually, we let this dog come into our house for a short time. We took it to the vet and then found it a special home with a boy that had just lost his special dog. This dog visited with Candy for a short time.

Two More Soon To Arrive

Then my husband and I decided to purchase two collie puppies. They were flown in from South Florida.

Candy was not well and Sammy our cat would hang out with her, keeping her company. The two puppies stayed close to Candy too.

Two puppies Maggie, Buddy and Candy

Candy and Sammy also

Candy Crosses The Rainbow Bridge

The night before Candy passed away. I sat up with her during the night and sang praise and worship songs like I had done so many times before when we lived in Wisconsin.

The next day just a couple of weeks before Christmas, Candy went to heaven, laying next to my husband by a small Christmas tree in our living room. I lost my very special friend, companion, and my ability to sing. I didn't sing again for over five years. The lost of Candy was a lot for me to bear.

My husband and I went to the beach for the day just after Candy went to heaven. We sat on the sand and I looked up to see a family with a dog. It was a collie. I couldn't believe my eyes. What were the chances of seeing a collie at the beach but there it sat right across from me? Oh, how I wanted to take that collie home, but of course I could not. But I had to go over and say hello.

Good thing we had two new baby collies. We named them Maggie and Buddy. And they became our new blessing from God. They were full of puppy love.

I was sad for many days after losing Candy. I would go out in the backyard in the morning and just stand there for a while with a saddened heart. But, one morning God showed me many birds. A tremendous group of birds flew overhead on my right, then another group on my left side and then even another group right over my head. God was showing me how he took care of all the animals and that Candy was with him. He spoke to my heart and said, "There is an abundance of life in my world."

I also went out in the back of our home one night and saw the most glorious sunset. It was another special blessing especially for me from God.

A Special Christmas Song

There was one song that I sang when I was sitting in a chair with Candy laying by me one Christmas day. We had been video taping so I still have this part on the tape. I was singing the song "I'll Be Home For Christmas". Every time I hear this song, I feel like she is letting me know she is there at Christmas time for me. Remember I told you how she came into my life a few weeks before Christmas and then twelve years later, a few weeks before Christmas, she went to heaven? Well, this has become my special song.

Candy I Love You.

You Are Always In My Heart

My Special Christmas Gift From God.

Candy Always In My Heart

How Long Oh Lord?

How long oh Lord, do I search for you in the midst of my feelings of sadness? Are you sitting in a season of time when your days roll into nights, and nights into days? When the difficulties of life keep rolling in like waves of the sea? Do you find yourself saying, "Where are you my Lord, my Savior? Why does this darkness cover my soul as a blanket, every day and every night?"

Yes, I have been there. You are not alone. I'd like to share with you how the Lord helped me to walk out of that time.

I was sitting in the waves of sorrow that were rolling in towards my soul. I went to my husband and he shared with me what he could from the Lord. My husband, basically said, "When you turn it over to the Lord, this time of darkness will end." Well, that's just great, I thought. I could try, but the waves of sadness hit so strong, knocking me from side to side. I didn't even have the ability to think faith. It was as if a person was swimming and the waves kept hitting and hitting. After a while the shoreline was not in clear sight.

God has his ways to help us. I purchased a cassette by Kenneth Copeland. The tape was full of songs that I hoped would bring me into a state of worship. All of a sudden, as I was listening to the tape, a song came on which confirmed what my husband had shared with me previously and further encouraged me to reach out to the Lord.

The special words in this particular song were **"how will it end, look to him"**. I played this song over and over to get it into my soul ... sometimes very loud to close out the voices urging me on to wallow in the unhappiness I was feeling.

Jesus said "I will never leave you or forsake you" God says, "See, I have engraved you in the palm of my hand".

One day as I was parking in a parking lot ready to go shopping it started to rain. As I sat in my car, with the rain pouring down on my windshield, tears started streaming down my face, God spoke to me and said, "The raindrops on your window are my angels crying for you today". I said, "Oh God, you have more to say to me, don't you?" I grabbed a pen and some paper from my purse and proceeded to pen what God spoke to my heart that day:

Teardrops From Heaven

The teardrops on your window
Are the teardrops from my angels
Crying for you …

To let you know you are not alone.
My tears fill your broken heart
And comfort you in this time of need.
They are tears from heaven
That flow from my throne
To let you know
That you are not alone.

For when you are saddened
My heart cries for you,
To send comfort to you.

Teardrops from heaven
For you this day
Streaks your window
Reflecting your inner cry of sadness.

My comfort to you this day
Are teardrops on your windshield.
Tears from heaven
To help wash away the sorrow.

Teardrops from heaven.
Teardrops as I cry for you
To let you know I am close
To healing your pain.

Teardrops from heaven
Teardrops from heaven.

By Marilyn Marinelli
(Given To Me From God)

Herein, began the healing of my soul. The waves became less and the faith and love of God started to grow again. I remembered Psalm 23 "The Lord is my Shepherd. The Lord is my Shepherd" … sometimes God will only give us a little bit of his word to strengthen us. Remember, "The Lord is my (your) Shepherd" too.

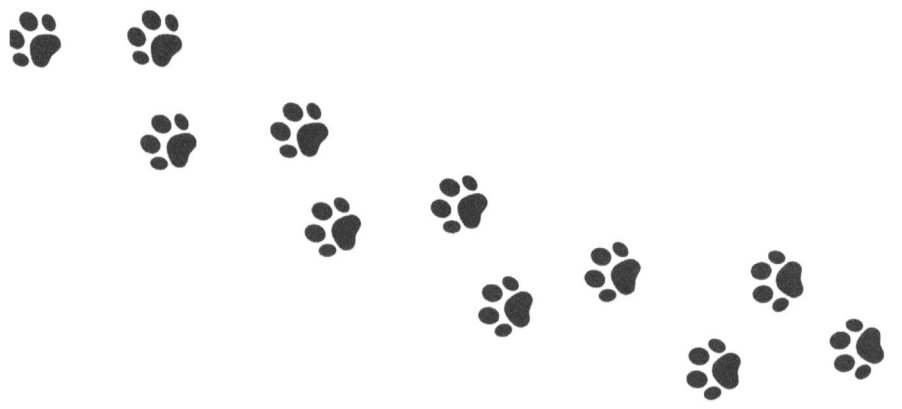

Chapter Two

Maggie And Buddy

Maggie and Buddy

The Closet Experience

NOW YOU HAVE TO UNDERSTAND that I am not a perfect Christian. Are you? If you are, you should think again, for no one is perfect, but Jesus.

Anyway, I have had a very hard time over the years. There was a time when I lived in sadness most every day, struggling with my walk with God, because of the enemy's attacks. It was as if every time I got up, I was spun around and punched. Men could relate when I say it was like being in a boxing match where things really get heated.

God is so good to us, when we don't give up. I felt I was hanging on with a thread somehow attached to God. Many things were attacking my walk with God, so that I would give up on following him. But, in my deep despair, I still called out to God for help and he answered my call.

I had to do some things, like make an effort to seek him and his Word, yet I couldn't read my Bible. I didn't want to sing praises. I didn't want to hear preaching and I didn't want to be around any Christians. That is how deep my despair was. Yet deep inside, I didn't want to walk away from God. Waves of darkness consumed my soul and fear tried to take hold. When I went to church, a song or a word of preaching spun me into tears of sadness. Needless to say, I was afraid to go to church, because I didn't want to cry any more.

What about my husband? Of course, he tried to share God's wisdom with me. I heard but couldn't apply things and I understood; yet the pull of sorrow became stronger. Mind you, I didn't want to run from God, but I guess I was running away from circumstances and thereby, I also found myself running away from God.

I realized finally, that I had a choice. There are always two roads to walk. You walk with God or walk away from God. After all the blessings I received and the times God has used me to minister to others, I really didn't want to give up my walk with him.

But sometimes, I am sorry to say, there are people around us that are Christians and yet are not really walking in God's love and wisdom, yet they think they are. These people can really trip you up. I urge you to watch out for them. Keep your walk with God and Stay in his Word.

Regardless of the circumstances, I tried to listen to Christian music and was blessed from time to time. Then I started to listen to TBN and God started speaking to me through Jan Crouch and her story of depression (great testimony), Kenneth Copeland, Creflo Dollar, Joyce Myers and a minister from Ft. Lauderdale, all of them unbelievably, preached on the same subject … Get Out of the boat and walk on the water to Jesus. Just reach out and Jesus will be there for you.

Finally, God's message got through to me and this is what happened. I pray I can express it all properly.

I had just listened to pastor Creflo Dollar preaching and said, "OK God, I am going in my room and get things in order with you." So I went in my room, took off my shoes and in my heart said, "God I'm coming to you and taking my shoes off like Moses did, so I can walk on Holy Ground." I sat down on my bed and put my Bible in front of me and prayed, "God I understand your message. I want to come back to you." Then I heard a faint cry of a cat (meow) and thought oh, another lost animal.

Let's Pause For A Station Break

I have to stop for a minute and tell you, not only through my time of sadness did I come across a lot of sad women, but also have helped rescue a few dogs and a cat. Almost every other week, when I would go out, I would see a lost dog… at least 5 in the past month. We don't live in the wilderness. There are many homes here so where were they coming from?

After the loss of my collie, Candy; many lost dogs seem to show up around my neighborhood. I even rescued several and found suitable homes for them. I began to visit the local Humane Society and found myself praying for many of the animals.

The loss of my beloved collie moved me to generally look at collie sites on the internet. In doing so, I started to learn more and more about rescue groups.

As I searched the net, it became clear to me that God was calling me to become involved in the "No Kill" movement and to join the rescue effort. My deep Christian faith and love for animals kept me ever searching and studying. I compiled all the date and adapted it to form the inter-workings of Have A Heart for Companion Animals.

Eventually me husband John joined me in the planning and set up of the agency. His prior knowledge of non-profit management, sales and marketing and public relations helped me to establish a strong foundation. Together, we established Have A Heart for Companion Animals, an animal welfare, rescue and referral non-profit organization www.haveaheart.us

My vision is to be a major influence and contributor to the elimination of euthanasia as a means of animal control. I believe that life is a gift from God, even animal life, and that the best animal shelter is a caring community.

*****Now back to my story*****

What? A Cat In My Closet.

To go on with what happened, I started to speak to God again, but I heard another cry of a cat (meow, meow). "Oh, it's my cat. He must have been shut up in the closet by accident." Sure enough, it was my cat, Sammy, that I heard crying and of course, I rescued him from his dilemma.

My two dogs, Buddy and Maggie came running in and jumped on the bed to see what was happening. They were rejoicing with me and began kissing Sammy. Why am I telling you this story? Where does God fit into this? Well, let me tell you the most remarkable thing.

The preacher I was listening to said, "Jesus has his hand reaching out to you. All you have to do is reach back and you can walk on the water with him and get out of the storm."

God revealed to me that since I reached out to him with understanding and made an effort to follow him, he was already there for me and was rejoicing that I had come back home to be with him.

Now let me tell you the funniest thing. God has a sense of humor and also uses things we can understand. Maggie and Buddy were jumping around with joy that Sammy was out of the closet. While I was rejoicing on getting Sammy, my cat, out of the darkness of the closet, God was showing me, in my spirit, how he was rejoicing over me, that I chose to reach out to him and he was taking me out of my closet of darkness. God's word from the Bible to me at that time was, Luke 19:10 "For the Son of man came to seek and to save that which was lost."

God showed me that my two dogs were rejoicing and wondering what was going on and kissing Sammy was a picture of God's angels rejoicing with him …that I had come back home to God. I laughed and laughed and laughed, how God could use this circumstance to show me his joy and now I found myself rejoicing and laughing with God.

Not only did God show me all this joy but he also allowed me a little of how much joy he had over me on my return. He did this every time I touched Sammy. A tremendous amount of joy would flow through me and God kept saying to my spirit, **"This is the joy I feel for you"**. Every time I touched my dogs, God allowed me to feel some of what he feels when he touches his Angels. God and me, laughed for a long time and joy returned back to my soul (mind, will and emotions).

I couldn't stop laughing for the longest time. My husband heard me and said, "Why are you laughing so much? I told him what happened and said, "God just placed this extraordinary joy all over me."

The next thing that happened was that my two dogs and I went out in the backyard and they ran and ran and ran with lots of life streaming in abundance. As I rejoiced in the backyard, thanking God, he spoke to my spirit again and said, ***"Life streams from me. There is an abundance of life in my world."***

All of a sudden Maggie was running and jumping and moving like Candy used to do. I couldn't believe my eyes. Another blessing.

II Corinthians 3:5 says…"Not that we are sufficient of ourselves to think of anything as being of ourselves, but our sufficiency is from God." And Psalms 66:5 says, "Come and see the works of God: He is awesome in his doing toward the sons of men."

The last scripture the Lord shared with me was Psalms 16:7…" Return to your rest oh my soul for the Lord has dealt bountifully with you."

Buddy And Maggie, A Special Pair

Things started to get better and I went on with my life with my kitty cat Sammy and my two new additions of love, Maggie and Buddy. My husband and I enjoyed watching them chase each other around the house. They would run around the kitchen area to the living room and then the hallway, Maggie first, Sammy in the middle and then Buddy pulling up the rear. It was funny to watch them chasing each other and having fun.

Here is a picture of my husband, Sammy, Maggie and Buddy by the fireplace.

John, Maggie, Buddy and Sammy

Buddy and Maggie had fun chasing each other around the back yard everyday. I would take each one out for a walk…one at a time. It was a special time with them. And of course, there were training classes.

Not All Trainers Are Alike

We decided to take Buddy and Maggie to a local pet store and use their trainer. Big mistake. I won't mention the name of the store but it was one of the big ones. This first time there a lady mentioned that her dog was from the shelter and her husband was fine with the dog but she wasn't so if she could learn how to work with the dog, she would keep it. Well, don't you know the next time we went for the first training course, this idiot trainer takes her dog as an example of how to teach your dog to sit.

Well, the dog didn't understand him and so it didn't sit. This guy held this poor dog up by the leash dangling it. Then he proceeded to tell the people this was how to deal with their dog if it didn't listen. I was extremely upset with this jerk and decided not to ever go back there again. I also put in a major complaint against him. Needless to say, we moved on to a kinder trainer. Every day I would walk Maggie and Buddy individually to practice sit, stay, come and walking on a leash. What good smart dogs they were.

What I have observed from our dogs is the excitement they express related to the questions that I ask them. They look and wonder, "Are we going with you today?" or "Do we stay home?" If I say, "Want to go for a walk or a ride in the van? They would jump with joy and run all over the house barking and barking, running and leaping with excitement and joy.

If they see me get dressed and I don't say a word, they wonder and hang around just waiting for the words ride or walk. If I say, "I'm going to the store", they just look as if to say, "Oh all right, guess we are not going anywhere." They don't realize they are better off at home but they respect me anyway. But when I do tell them to come with me, they are protected by me, even if they think they have it all together.

When my puppy dogs, Maggie and Buddy, obey what I ask them to do, they also find provisions. Their water is always available, they always have food, and they are always sitting under the protection of my love. If they didn't, they would wander off on their own, searching for something to eat and something to drink, never finding peace and always searching for comfort and love.

As we all know, everyone that they would come across would not treat them so kindly. After all, there are many dangers out there. Good thing they have learned to obey me and respect me. Then they will be protected, provided for and loved. Who wouldn't want to have that? By the way, my dog Buddy just loved watching T.V., especially Animal Planet. He just sat there in an overstuffed chair with his front paws crossed and didn't have a care in the world. Why? Because, he knew in whom he believes. He trusted me and felt safe.

(Picture #14) Buddy sitting in the big chair

Well, how much more will our Father, God take care of us if we will seek him and heed his voice. When God says, **"WALK"** then we walk. When he says, **"STAY",** then we stay and when he says, **"COME"**, then we come… All the time knowing we are in his care, love and protection.

Our Virginia Experience

My husband and I decided to move again, this time to the state of Virginia. This was a place he spent his childhood and thought it would be fun. It was a change for Buddy and Maggie and of course Sammy, our cat. There was a new backyard for Buddy and Maggie to run around. There was a friendly neighbor's cat that would come over the fence and visit Maggie and Buddy everyday. Maggie just would be kind but Buddy and the kitty cat would hang out together. There was also the visit from the new growing puppy that the neighbor let out on its own everyday.

The puppy would come by our fence and I would give Buddy and Maggie and the puppy a treat every morning. Buddy and Maggie didn't like the cars and sometimes a truck passing along the road in front of our house. Even though the road was pretty far away. They just didn't really appreciate the sound of them passing by. They did enjoy the snow. The snow was a new thing for them since we lived in Florida where there was no snow.

Oh Deer Me

Maggie and I had an unusual experience one afternoon. I decided to take her to PetSmart for a ride and to walk the store and shop for something special for her and Buddy. But, oh no, it could never be. I was driving on a 4-lane road with a median between on the way to the store. "Oh look Maggie, a deer running across the road."

Somehow or another the deer ran in front of where I was driving and I grabbed the steering wheel, holding on real tight and prayed. As I kept my eyes shut real tight anticipating the impact of hitting the deer but nothing happened. I opened my eyes in relief that there was no deer to be seen. But, all of a sudden bam! The deer hit my windshield right in front of me. What a horrible sight. I was filled with fear stopped my car and tried to get out but my door wouldn't open. So, I got out from the passenger side. I looked around and saw a police car. The policeman took me into his patrol car with a man that was driving a truck.

The policeman asked the driver of the truck what happened. The truck driver told him that he hit the deer and it went about 20 feet in the air. Then it came down on my car. I felt frightened and sad. I spoke with the officer for a while till my husband came to get me. My car was smashed from the driver's side to the front window.

Poor Maggie! I checked on her and she seemed to be all right and not showing any sign of fear. We both got into my husband's car and went home. Of course, we got our car fixed, but I was upset for quite a while after this incident.

Christmas came and went and we all had a wonderful time celebrating the holiday together.

Me, Buddy and Maggie

We learned that there were many deer out in the area where we lived. We would come home in the evening and see deer in our front yard. Sometimes driving down the road during the day, many of them would be crossing the street and cars would stop to let them go over to the other side.

Moving On To Lakeland

We didn't live in Virginia for long and decided to sell our house and move back to Florida. There was another new home to explore. Maggie and Buddy and Sammy had a lot of van riding. They were really good at it too. Next home we lived in was in Lakeland, Florida. Come on Buddy, Maggie and Sammy, let's all move back to Florida where it was warmer.

There was another opportunity of a new porch and backyard to explore for the fur family. Buddy and Maggie would go for walks with me around the neighborhood. They had a new yard to go out and play in and Sammy had a new porch to hang around outside everyday.

Something Strange Happened

One day after our dogs got their Rabies shots. Something strange happened to Maggie. I went out in the backyard to bring the dogs in and Maggie rolled on her back which was her way of saying, "I don't think I want to go in right now." As I looked down at her I noticed a lot of black and blue bruises on her stomach. I thought, "What in the world was this?" My two dogs never fight or play rough with each other. So, what is going on? Right away I told my husband and we decided to have Maggie looked at by a different vet.

The vet I found was a lady vet, Dr. Brimcomb. She had been on Animal Planet. I assumed she would be someone good to take Maggie too. So come on Maggie, let's get in the car and go to the vet. On the way there, I saw a truck that was pulling a flat bed filled with logs, cut from trees. All of a sudden, the logs started to drop off the flat bed. WOW, I thought. "What to do." Thank God I was able to sway away from the logs rolling down the road in my direction.

Finally, Maggie and I arrived at the vets' office. While waiting in the waiting room I learned that people came from all over Florida to bring their dogs to her. She specialized in dealing with pregnant dogs.

We were called into a room to be seen by the vet. She took a look at Maggie, gave her some kind of blood test right there and came back with the results. The vet proceeded to tell me that if I hadn't brought Maggie in that day, she would have died the next day. Her platelets had dropped extremely low. The vet gave Maggie a shot. She told me to keep bringing Maggie in every week to have her tested to see if her platelets were coming up.

Weeks passed and every week I took Maggie to the vet, praying every time that she would be getting better. Maggie did get better but no more Rabies shots for her. My prayer was answered and Maggie was able to go on with her life.

We went to so many places. We would all go to the local park. We would visit my husband's mother. At Christmas time, we would take rides around the neighborhood and see the beautiful Christmas lights.

Me, Sammy the cat, Buddy, Maggie by the Christmas Tree

I know we have moved a lot and you may wonder why. We could move and not worry about my husband's job since he was able to work from home. This made it easy for us. He called the different moves, "Working Vacations." We were able to see a lot of places in each state. So really; it has been lots of fun.

Moving On, Again

Ocala, Florida was the next stop. Maggie, Buddy and Sammy moved with us from Lakeland to Ocala. What can I say? another nice big back yard and another porch for Sammy and for all of us to enjoy. We named the porch "Sammy's Porch" since he loved to spend his days lying around outside and enjoying the sun.

Sammy on his porch

Maggie and Buddy would take a walk with me almost every day. They would run the backyard and enjoyed being groomed every Sunday. I did the grooming. It was a pleasant time.

My husband and I would take Maggie and Buddy to a special park and also to one that was closer to where we lived.

Every Christmas, my husband and I would take Maggie and Buddy in the van and ride through the neighborhood to see all the terrific Christmas displays.

Buddy was a big rough collie almost all black with touches of white. He was so handsome. He loved sitting on the big chair in our living room and watching T.V. He was a gentle soul. He was kind, easy going with a heart full of love. Yes, he was Maggie's special friend too. They came from the same mommy dog. We spent many years together with Buddy, Maggie and Sammy.

Buddy Sitting On The Chair

A Major Recall And What Happened

Around the time that Buddy and Maggie were about 10 ½ years old, there was a major recall on dog food. Many, many different brands of dog food were destroying dog's lives.

I opened a new dog food bag. It didn't look right. There were two different colored kibbles. I didn't know what was going on yet and fed some of it to Buddy and Maggie. I called the company that made this brand of dog food and they told me to get a new bag and they would pay for it. So, I bought a new bag and it still didn't look right. So, I bought a different dog food. Well, what ever was in this original dog food already started something that couldn't be stopped in effecting my two dogs.

I soon learned, but not soon enough, that there was a MAJOR RECALL ON DOG FOOD. Many different makes were being recalled. What a horrible time for all the dog owners.

My two dogs started to lose their ability to bark like normal and their noses started to turn more reddish pink and not black looking anymore.

I took them both to the vet and told the vet what happened. He didn't do much but did say that Maggie had a lump on her tail and it was cancerous. I allowed them to do surgery on her but that didn't help her for long. The vet didn't know what to do about the barking problem.

I took Buddy to a different vet and they did a test on him and told us that he had cancer. In the meantime, my cat Sammy got sick. I took him to the vet and found out his kidneys were failing. It wasn't an easy time for them or us.

I went out one night with my husband and the strangest thing happened. I was sitting around with a lot of people when I sensed so strong the presence of Maggie very near me and passing by me. I can't really explain it but it was a very, very different feeling. Like she was letting me know she was leaving.

We came home that night and Maggie had passed away in our living room. The next morning our cat Sammy passed away. A few weeks later Buddy passed away.

I can't tell you how crazy this all was. In the meantime, I was learning all about the recalls on dog food. It had been getting worse and worse and worse. Well, I lost all three, Buddy, Maggie and Sammy. It was one of the saddest times of my life.

I came across two little statues one of a black collie like Buddy and one sable like Maggie. I also came across a small statue of a white cat that looked like Sammy with his paw up in the air like Sammy used to do when he would sit on our kitchen table on a napkin waiting for some treat. I placed them on my kitchen counter top and they are still there as a tribute to my beloved collies and blessed cat.

My Loving Three - Ceramic Statues

My Loving Three
That Were A Blessing From God
Our Home was for them To Be Together
and Live Their Lives Protected and Loved.

Chapter 3

Rubydoobee, My Collie Girl Always In My Heart

WHERE DO I BEGIN? AT the beginning of course. It seems quite logical to start there, doesn't it?

Ruby's birth was in April when all the flowers bloomed. And so it was that she was born and blossomed into a wonderful beautiful collie girl puppy.

There was her picture in the ad. The ad read collie puppies for sale.

Collie Puppy Ad Showing Ruby

Well, before we knew it, my husband and I were on the road to see the puppies. As we arrived, we were greeted by one collie mommy dog, one border collie mommy dog and one beautiful handsome male collie dog and of course, a bunch of puppies.

Which ones to chose? My husband had his eye on a wonderful little border/collie mix male puppy. My husband saw a little one that looked like the runt of the litter and his heart went out to him.

One lady seemed interested in another boy puppy. My husband said, "I hope she takes that one." Sure enough, she decided to…so my husband picked up our new little boy puppy. He was the runt of the litter.

I wanted a collie girl puppy and there she was, the only sable collie girl left and she just had to be mine.

Soon our two new additions were riding in our van on the way home to live with us. As I turned to look from our van leaving the property, the mommy collie and the daddy collie were watching from the fenced backyard. My heart went out to them. They were watching two of their babies leave on a new journey.

On our ride home we stopped at a friend's home to show them our new puppies. They loved on the pups for a while and then we went on our way.

Home at last, we arrived with our two new wonderful puppies.

Kody and Ruby Playing With My Shoe

What To Name Them

Months before we bought our two new dogs, my husband kept kidding around saying, "We should call our next female dog Ruby." He would kid around every so often saying, "Ruby, want to play checkers?" He would say this about three times in a row and every time we would both start laughing.

I desperately tried other names like Missy, or any other name but Ruby, but those other names never seemed to fit this little girl puppy. Ruby was the name. It just seemed right. My husband named our puppy boy Kody. Yep. Ruby and Kody were what we named them.

Ruby was a beautiful, sweet, funny and inquisitive collie pup. She was my "collie girl" that ran the yard every day chasing squirrels with her brother Kody. That was their job. Kody never missed a day to give Ruby kisses. What a loving dog he was to her.

Kody Kissing Ruby

After a while, I changed Ruby's name to Ruby Doobee, lol. Sometimes I called her Ruby and others just Doobee. She came to both when I called.

Ruby and Kody ate and played together right from the start, chasing each other around the backyard. Yes, they were meant to be together, running around and sharing life.

Kody and Ruby Running In The Backyard

Training Time

Of course, there was training time for the both of them. So, there we were, the four us in the van. There I was driving, my husband keeping an eye on the puppies and Ruby and Kody barking their little hearts out the whole time. Every time we went out riding in the van they would bark and we would yell at them to be quite…this never worked. I think they thought we were barking with them. How funny is that?

We went to class and met other puppies in training. My Ruby stood out from the crowd. She was the friendly one, wanting to say hello to the other puppies and their owners.

The trainer called her, "The Class Clown," but she really wasn't. She was just a friendly outgoing puppy with lots of energy and love. She was full of life and I loved her for that.

After one of the training sessions, we were allowed to put Ruby and Kody in a gated area at the training park. They loved it, but a lady put her puppy in there with them and it didn't know how to run and play.

Ruby and Kody were wild and crazy and loved to enjoy life. This lady got scared and pulled her puppy out. Too bad, maybe this little one would have had some fun. Oh well.

Ruby, Kody and me had some good times together, lots of love and kisses. I put leis around their necks and scarf's just for fun.

Kody and Ruby with playing with the leis)

Kody loved to catch balls and freebees. Just throw it and he would run and fetch it, or catch it in his mouth. He was full of life and very loving. He also loved to dance around with me when I put music on.

Ruby, on the other hand, wanted to watch everything. She patrolled the backyard and front of the house. She loved getting up on the love seat and look out the window to see what was happening.

The backyard was their time to chase the many squirrels that tried to come in our yard. Oh, how I loved them both. They were a team for sure. They never caught a squirrel but it was fun to watch them try.

You see, we had lost our previous two collie dogs to cancer, so Ruby and Kody were very special.

I would lay down most every afternoon for a nap and John, my husband, would put Ruby and Kody on the bed with me to comfort me. That is how they learned that getting on the bed with us was fun and they got a lot of loving. So, every morning, as they got older, Ruby would jump up on the bed and then Kody to get some special time of love.

Ruby became the more dominant collie. Kody was always giving her kisses. What a loving dog. Almost everyday, Kody was there, showing her love. They were a great team.

Birthdays came and went and each time we had a birthday I would put birthday hats on me, my husband and them. We would sing happy birthday and have a ton of fun.

A Challenge of Faith

Spay and neuter day came. One day, after Ruby was spayed, things changed. She was put on antibiotics, one after another, but they didn't clear up anything. She couldn't keep her food digested, was losing weight and losing her strength. The vet didn't know what to do anymore.

Then our vet said she would give Ruby one more test called a TLI test. The test came out positive. My Ruby had EPI, (Exocrine Pancreatic Insufficiency). This is a disease of the pancreas. Her pancreas stopped working and wasn't producing enzymes to digest her food. This would cause a dog or yes even a person to starve to death. Not a good prognosis.

I asked the vet "What do I do?" The vet said she only had one dog like that and the owner said it died from a snake bite.

NO, NOT MY RUBY GIRL… SHE IS NOT GOING TO DIE, I thought.

My vet had me start her on the powder form of enzymes. That would replace the enzymes needed for her body to digest food. She couldn't handle it and I was allergic to it. She was getting sicker… my poor, poor baby. My vet didn't know what more to do. I saw Ruby not even 6 months old so weak, losing weight, and not being able to digest her food. She was slowly dying before my eyes.

Someone else might have decided this would be the end of this precious puppy but

NOT ME. OH NO, NOT ME. I PRAYED FOR DIRECTION AND HELP.

After praying about the situation, I came across "EPI 4 Dogs" on the Internet. God dropped a lifeline into our path. I read and read and researched and asked questions. I was determined to help Ruby Doobee live.

I learned a lot. I started her on Creon capsules, an enzyme replacement. When it became too expensive to buy it locally, I found an online source where I could buy them cheaper from Canada.

I bought her special enzymes that would help dogs with EPI to digest their food easily. Then I added, B-12 with intrinsic factor twice a day to her food. I also started giving her Primal Defense, a probiotic.

This probiotic helped to eliminate the bad bacteria that had accumulated in her body from so many antibiotics.

I also bought special food for her and had to learn to balance the capsules of Creon with how much food I gave her twice a day. A challenge? Yes, but Ruby was going to live. I am not giving up and I am not stopping my prayers and my research.

I was now on "Poop Patrol" as the EPI 4 dogs folks called it. I was checking to make sure what I was doing for Ruby was working.

I kept daily records on what I was doing for Ruby so that I would know what to change or not.

It wasn't easy but I was determined that Ruby would live.

Things Were Getting Better

Ruby Doobee lived but I still had challenges to keep her going. I spoke with 3 vets but they didn't know much. I could have taught all three of them. So, it was… God, Me, Ruby Doobee, and the EPI family. It worked well.

Ruby started gaining weight and loved to eat again. She was filled with energy once again, running with her brother Kody Oodee. lol

They chased each other and patrolled the backyard, keeping the squirrels out, just like before.

Ruby Doobee took her role back as the leader. She had a mind of her own but respected me. She started jumping up on the bed in the mornings and taking afternoon naps with me once again. What a cuddle bug.

Ruby Was Honored

In June 2016, Ruby was a part of "EPI Microbiome Fecal Matter Research study. She was chosen from many other EPI dogs because she was doing so extremely well in living regardless of this disease.

This study was done by:

EPI 4 DOGS Foundation, Inc. And

Dr. Suchodolski Med Vet,

Dr Vet Med, Pd, AGAF, DACVM,

Texas A&M Gastrointestinal Laboratory

College Station, Texas, USA

Ruby was also featured in one of the EPI calendars. They named the page "Marilyn's Ruby". This was the picture that was in the calendar.

Picture of Ruby in the EPI 4 Dogs Calendar

Ruby Doobee was nosey. She had to check out everything. She wanted to go for rides in the van, go for walks, get up on the loveseat, and look out the window and watch what might be going on outside. She was my blessing and I was hers. We had lots of love and laughs with Ruby and Kody.

Ruby loved to bark and barked at almost everything, especially when going for rides in our van. It was as if she was saying hello to everything and everybody. *"Hello World."*

Ruby had her special ways of letting us know she had to go outside to do her business. She would either nudge you with her nose, or push the phone receiver off the hook in the middle of the night.

The phone would make a beep, beep, beep sound that would always wake one of us up. During the day she would run to the door and look at us like, "Well, are you going to let me out?"

She loved to eat and would even go after Kody's food until I would tell her no and to leave his food alone. She never really learned to stay away from his food so it was almost like a game.

Ruby Doobee was challenged with health problems and yet she had the desire to live life to the fullest. She was a special needs dog that surmounted all odds to live a full life. Her life was filled with love and giving love and she was able to share it all with us.

A favorite time for her was to chew ice cubes. I would shake the ice cubes in the freezer and she would come running. "Give me ice cubes", she seemed to say. Crunch, crunch she would eat sometimes 4 of them. Of course, Kody got some too, but he had to watch out for Ruby coming his way to try and steal his ice cubes.

When we were in the living room, watching T.V., she would curl up between the sofa and the loveseat near the end table.

Day after day we would enjoy each other's company. She was my special collie girl, full of love and life. I couldn't have asked for a more special loving dog.

Expectations

The expectations of the creatures wait for the
sons of God, relying on their faith.

For the creature was made subject to man's vanity, not
willingly but still waiting for what is to be.

The creature itself shall also be,
delivered from bondage into God's liberty.

Romans 8:19-21

Written By Marilyn Marinelli

Years Past And Things Changed

When Ruby was 10 ½ years old things started to change. Some things weren't right with her. I didn't know what to do. My vet was on vacation; my husband was in the hospital in ICU with the Covid 19 virus. The emergency vets were extremely expensive.

Ruby was still eating and doing things but not the same. Then one afternoon, she ran out from the porch to chase a squirrel with her brother, Kody and she collapsed in the middle of the yard.

I tried to get her up but she couldn't walk, so I picked her up. God gave me the strength. I say that because I had been in ICU and rehabilitating and was not totally recovered from Ketoacidosis, and a diabetic coma.

But GOD gave me the strength to pick up Ruby Doobee and carry her on to my porch where she laid with her head on my lap for a long while. I later carried her to my bedroom and put her on her blanket.

I touched her face. I then placed a stuffed squirrel by her and said, "Ruby, you finally caught that squirrel." Ruby passed away lying next to me by my bed.

Ruby Is Now Safe in Jesus's Arms

Ruby Doobee lived 10 ½ years. A Collie's life span would be about 10-14 years. She still lived a life with love to give and love to receive. She had a blessed life.

I miss her with all my heart. I believe she is in heaven and that Jesus held her close when she left my side.

My Little Collie Girl Now Lives with Jesus

A dedication is in Ruby's honor on the EPI website under "Memorials". I also received a wonderful card from Olesia, the Founder of www.EPI4dogs.org Enclosed in the card was a poem. It went like this…

The Moment That You Left Me

My heart split in two,
One side filled with memories,
The other side died with you.

I often lay awake at night when the
World is fast asleep, and take a
Walk down memory lane with
Tears upon my cheek.

I hold you tightly within my heart
And there you will remain.
You see life has gone on
Without you, but will
Never be the same.

RUBY DOOBEE ALWAYS IN MY HEART AND MIND

Ruby Doobee Always In My Heart and Mind

In Loving Memory to Rubydoobee

Marilyn Marinelli

cpoets@embarqmail.com

I saw a picture of Jesus holding a dog.

The caption under the picture read,

"Welcome Home"

My Special Thanks

Thank you, God that helped Ruby to live; To all the people that have helped through the years, Olesia the founder of EPI 4 dogs first and foremost and then to all from around the world that gave me direction, help and encouragement.

Thank you to those that do all the research about EPI and have given me input… you have been a blessing to my beautiful "collie girl" and me. I Thank You!

Chapter Four

Nellie, A New Beginning

Nellie

My Story Doesn't End Here. It actually is a new beginning.

Nellie, the Collie, came up on my Facebook page months after Ruby went to heaven. The picture of the collie was beautiful and the eyes moved and so did the mouth and this was the song she sang. I felt like God sent it to me so that I would know that Ruby was all right and cared about me. I shed many tears but what a blessing this song was to me.

Here are the words to the song "Good Morning Sung By Nellie the Collie

> Good Morning! Good Morning
> The Best To You This Morning
> How Are You? How Are You?
> I Hope You're Feeling Fine
> And Happy All The Time.

> Good Morning! Good Morning
> The Best To You This Morning
> How Are You? How Are You?
> I Hope You're Feeling Fine
> And Happy All The Time.

> Hummmmm

It is a new beginning with Nellie, the puppy collie girl that is now in my life. Thank you, God, for making a way where there was no way and a path where there was no path.

You see, God showed me a scripture in the Bible weeks ago that "faith is the substance of things hope for the and evidence of things not yet seen." I have been trusting God through my faith that he would provide and that faith has been used as the substance of things hoped for (a new collie girl) and the evidence of things not ye seen.

I told God, "If I get another collie puppy, I would name her Nellie because of the song I heard from Nellie the Collie facebook post. Many days later, I saw Jesus' hands and arms stretched out to me from his gown with a collie puppy. I believed that my new collie girl was going to be provided to me from God.

So, I waited, but not for long. I went on facebook one day and there on Ocala 4 sale was posted a collie puppy for sale. We didn't have the money but somehow along the way the money was available to us and we called and went to pick up our new puppy girl.

God provided a door to be opened for me to receive a blessing. When I realized that this puppy would be mine, I cried a zillion tear. I cried for the loss of Rubydoobee and also cried for the overwhelming feeling that God would bless me with a special collie puppy.

Someone said to me before this blessing took place that "Grief was there because love had no place to go." Well now my grief of losing Rubydoobee would be changed into a new collie girl named Nellie. My love now would have a place to go.

I sang the song, "Nellie The Collie", to my Nellie, the new little collie puppy every morning.

One day after I got Nellie, I went to the supermarket to get some groceries and when I went to get eggs. I saw the writing on a carton of eggs that was written "Nellie's Eggs" I couldn't believe what I was seeing the words Nellie on a carton of eggs. I thought wait until I tell my husband about this and purchased the carton to show my husband. Since then, I buy the Nellie eggs. What a conformation.

Why is Nellie a blessing to me was something I will share with you now, but first, I need to tell you what happened before I got her so you will understand the importance of her in my life.

I had been in the hospital before I was blessed with Nellie. One night I was taken to the hospital by my husband and was totally out of it. I had been placed in ICU because I had gone into a coma and had ketoacidosis, which was caused by diabetes that I had been dealing with. I also had pneumonia and my kidneys were failing. The doctor told my husband that he should prepare himself for the worst. That I might not survive.

Well, my husband made calls to everyone he knew that would pray for me. He also spoke to God and told him that he could take me home but that he really would like me to live and have me with him.

God allowed me to live, but the days I went through in the hospital were very traumatic. Then I was sent to a rehab facility. That two was difficult for me. I don't remember a lot of what I went through in the hospital or in rehab just bits and pieces.

I spent 15 days all alone with no visitors and some phone calls from my husband when I was in rehab. I wasn't allowed visitors because of the covid virus and the hospital and the rehab I was in were protecting their patients.

So, as a result, I didn't know what happened to me. No one told me anything when I was in the hospital. They just did their medical thing to help me live. In rehab, they didn't share any information with me on why I was there either. My husband had to tell me and help me when I got home from rehab.

Needless to say, I was traumatized from the whole thing. I came home to a new way of eating and living with lots of medication and tried to take care of myself. My husband helped me a lot and watched over me and helped me get moving again. He took me for rides in the van to go to the stores and sat in the van everyday as I walked the supermarket for exercise. He also helped me to start driving again with him sitting next to me.

I went in the hospital April 2020; Got out fifteen days later and by September 2020 I was off all medication. My doctor calls me a miracle.

But oh no, things didn't get all together better. In September, I took my husband to the ER and they sent him to the hospital. He had the covid virus. He was placed in ICU where he spent 18 days.

There I was taking care of myself, driving to see him but could only talk to him on the phone in the hospital and see him through a window. I was tested for the virus and it was positive but I only ran a slight fever and quarantined myself as needed.

So, there I was just getting better and my husband went into the hospital fighting for his life. He was sent home after 23-days. We went through the process with physical therapy, nurses, etc. as I did weeks before. I became his nurse and caregiver. He was on oxygen for many days as well.

Why am I telling you all this? Because then you can see why Nellie is S-o-o-o-o-o important. She keeps me active and focused and that is really important.

My dog Ruby wasn't doing very well. You remember she was my special needs dog that

died at 10 ½ years old. Well, to add on to everything else, one day my dog Kody saw a squirrel that was on the fence and went after it as he always would do with Ruby.

This time Ruby didn't make it and collapsed in the yard. That night Ruby left this world and went to heaven. I can't tell you how much I had cried. I had no one to help me. Go out for a cup of coffee or be with me as a support of any kind. It was tough.

I missed Ruby so much and after all I went through and was going through. My husband suggested we get another collie. This is the reason Nellie entered my life. She, hopefully, will be my, "Emotional Support Dog" because after all that I shared with you I came down with PTSD "Post Traumatic Stress Disorder". However, God is my provider and the one I look to for strength and direction.

A Little About Nellie Belly

Nellie is very unique. She is now a year old and just a beauty as you can see in her picture below.

Nellie at a year old

Nellie has brought life into our lives. She is a challenge in everyway. She is a very pushy, demanding puppy girl. She wants to know everything and is determined to get her way.

She has been a forceful friend to my older dog Kody. He is 12 years old and has a difficult time getting up and even unstable sometimes on his feet, but she loves him and wants to play all the time with him. She just doesn't get it that he is too old for her to play with. She tugs on his ear and his hair and brings him toys to get him going but he does get up and move around and then let's her know he is not interested. I have to constantly tell her to leave Kody alone so we have to keep him separate from her so he gets to relax and be himself.

I couldn't take her to puppy class because of Covid at first. Then Petco's trainer quit. Then they got a new trainer but this person even though had been training for 21 years had to go through Petco's training class. This would be for a few more months before they would have any training lessons available.

Next, I was able to take her to a very well know training facility. First day there was our last day there. The trainer was unprepared with how to deal with a friendly puppy.

Nellie wanted to say hi to all the other dogs. So, she whined, and whined for a short time and the trainer told me to take her outside. The trainer never came to speak with me and just let me wonder what to do. We left very disturbed with her inability to deal with a young puppy.

One other trainer that I contacted was an excellent trainer that we used years ago with our other two puppies. Well, wouldn't you know it she sold her land where she trained and was looking to work and give lessons in her backyard of her home. But then she decided not to do lessons yet because new neighbors moved in and she was concerned that the training of puppies would bother them. Waiting some more …..She then called and let me know that she would be holding classes in her backyard. But now Nellie couldn't attend because she was scheduled to be spayed and that would take a couple of weeks for her to heal.

All this time it worked into one year of trying to find a place that held training lessons. So, I started to train her myself a little at a time between trying to find a trainer. Sit, stay, come, and walk on a leash.

Well, back to our home front. Nellie, loves her Nyla Bone, ball, pull toys and more.

She is a warm and cuddly puppy girl and loves to sit on the couch with us. Yes, with us isn't that cozy???? Lol She pushes open any door in the house if it's closed and there she is. Hi, I am here. Lol

Nellie Belly, we sometimes affectionately call her, is certainly a breath of fresh air here in our home. She is a real handful.

Holes, yes holes in various places in our backyard. Ooops don't step there. So, now I fill holes and put a fence around them so she won't go back and make them bigger. Of course, I fill the holes back up with whatever dirt is around, except for one by the drainage I really needs some extra soil. Well, we are working on that.

Nellie Belly really keeps us up and running. She loves to play, not only with us but also with Kody, our older dog. Poor Kody, she is forever bugging him to play with her by putting her butt up in the air as dogs do when they want to play. She tugs on his ear and sometimes tries to pull him around with some fur from his neck area.

Poor Kody, he is a 12-year-old border/collie mix and is having some problem getting up from time to time and doesn't have the ability to move as easy as he used to. But there is Nellie getting him going as she tries to let him know that he isn't all that bad off. She also shows him affection, kisses him and lies next to him. I would say she is good for him in his old age. She brings life into his world. If she gets too bothersome he just starts crying out and well then she cries out and me and my husband cry out "Nellie, leave Kody alone lol. Sometime it can be quite crazy in our home.

Nellie is very demanding and tries so hard to get her way. She is headstrong and a handful and very smart. But if I start to cry, she will come over and give me kisses. How sweet she can be. She just wants to be a part of the family and she is.

Alert as a watchdog? yep. Any sound that is out of the ordinary, there she is letting us know something is not right. All in all, she is a blessing to our home and brings life into our lives yes, including Kody. Did I mention I sometimes call Kody lovingly Kody Oodee?

Oh, there she goes again wanting the attention, love and affection that she so desperately deserves and needs. Kisses and hugs… Nellie you are a handful but a blessing to us all.

Bow wow. Oh, better not do that or she will be right there with a ball or bone in her mouth to play with me. Oh, I better hide. Why? because sometimes we just all need a break and some rest. Lol

Nellie is a blessing to all of us and is a great addition to our family. She is loved, cuddled, played with and cherished. She is the one that keeps me focused in the present and gives me kisses to let me know she cares for me. I look forward to many years with Nellie at my side.

Conclusion

I thank the Lord for all the love and blessings brought to me from the lives of your precious souls: Candy, Maggie and Buddy, Rubydoobee and Kodyodee, my collies and my kitty cats Snowball, Crystal and Sammy. I also give praise to God for allowing me to be Nellie's collie mom. She is my newest "Collie Girl."

Being a fur baby parent is the best thing that has ever happened to me. It taught me how to be longsuffering and understanding. It kept me focused and alert to the moment as well as sensitive to the needs of the future.

My Collie Girls are an embodiment of all the hopes and dreams of the future, the fond memories of the past, and the pure joy of the moment.

I THANK YOU FOR BEING A PART OF MY LIFE AND SHARING YOUR LIVES WITH ME.

YOU ARE FOR EVER LIVING IN MY HEART

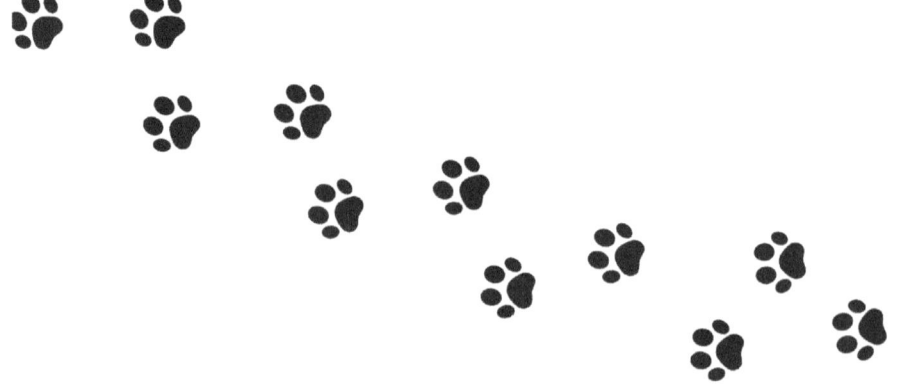

About the Author

Marilyn Marinelli

Marilyn Marinelli is an "Ordained Minister" of the gospel of Jesus Christ, associated with Faith Christian Fellowship Int'l, a worldwide full gospel fellowship. She is also Co-Author of "Together Forever" a marital enrichment home seminar.

She ministered for the Fellowship of Christian Poets for over 10 years through a monthly blog called "Ministry for the Poets Soul". She has ministered in song at various churches.

She is also the Founder and President of Have A Heart for Companion Animals, Inc. a ministry dedicated to the protection of companion animals. www.haveaheart.us

She has also played an important part in sharing information and statistics with the local county commissions to change the law regarding the chaining of dogs in her local county. No longer do dogs have to suffer that abuse.

She is the author of two published Christian books; titled "A Dry And Thirsty Land" and "Believing God" which are books that minister to women. Both share true victories in her walk with the Lord. They are currently being offered through www.marinellichristianbooks.com. "My Collie Girls And Me" is her third book in print.

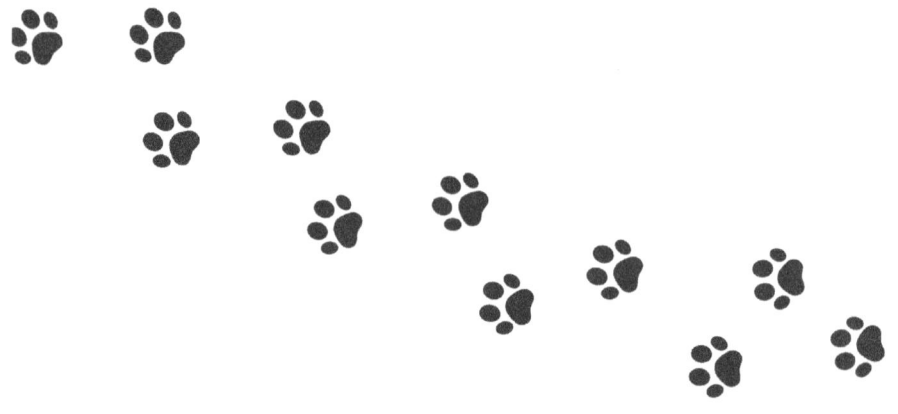

Selected Poetry By Marilyn Marinelli

Through The Eyes of A Stray Lost And Abandoned

I'm lost. I'm abandoned,

I am the eyes that look at you every day.

I am the one that looks at you through cages,

And waits for a kind word.

Water, food and just maybe your hand to touch me

So I can feel a little secure,

That my loneliness and fear

Would subside for just a little while.

I am the lost. I am the abandoned,

I am the eyes that look at you everyday.

I come to you filthy, scared, and bewildered.

I come to you in all shapes and sizes

I come to you with a broken heart

And yet still trust that maybe,
Just maybe, you will understand my plight.
I am the lost. I am the abandoned,
I am the eyes that look at you everyday.

Teach me, and be with me
And don't let them say I am shy or too dirty.
Teach me and I will be most loving and kind.
Don't say like you have said too many times,
"There is not enough room and we don't have the time."

Please set an example and let others know that I am worthy.
If you don't set the example how will others know?
I am the lost. I am the abandoned;
I am the eyes that look at you every day.

If you hold me so precious within your sight,
Others will see me and it will work out alright.
Don't you know, don't you see?
My heart is breaking … please help me.

Don't do as before and say it is all right.
It never will be if you take my life.
I am the lost. I am the abandoned;
I am the eyes that look at you every day.

Keep me out of the cage; give me a nice place to stay
I am not a criminal. I just went astray.

Keep me out of the cage; give me a nice place to stay
My heart is breaking because my owners left me today.

I am the lost. I am the abandoned;
I am the eyes that look at you every day.

Written By Marilyn Marinelli, President
Have A Heart for Companion Animals, Inc.
Ocala, Florida cpoets@embarqmail.com

Quiet Hours

In the silence of the quiet hours,
In the presence of a new dawn,
I bow down upon my knees,
For bringing me life reborn.

Taking off all the shackles,
Letting my spirit free,
I give all the thanks to Jesus,
For giving His love to me.

By Marilyn Marinelli

www.ingramcontent.com/pod-product-compliance
Lightning Source LLC
Chambersburg PA
CBHW051553010526
44118CB00022B/2685